When the renovated Louvre opens to the public,
I. M. walks through the courtyard deep in thought.
As he nears the entrance,
he is surprised by the loud applause of visitors,
French and foreign, who recognize him.
Behind his round glasses, I. M.'s eyes sparkle,
much like the sunbeams reflected by the pyramid.
He smiles broadly, nods to the crowd,
and walks on.

Soon after, the French president is reelected and the stunning new pyramid completed.

During the underground excavation, the thrilling discovery of castle walls, a moat, and hidden treasures leads I. M. Pei's team to open up these spaces for visitors to walk through and experience.

Issues arise. Solutions are found.

How can the glass be made without a green tint?
   A French company develops a special furnace.

How can the 673 glass panes be connected?
   An American maker of yacht rigging
   designs a spiderweb of metal cables to support
   the panes shaped like diamonds and triangles.

How will the panes be cleaned?
   Mountain climbers on ropes will use sponges and squeegees.

I. M. is onsite during every stage.
But he worries that if the president isn't reelected,
a new president might stop the pyramid project.
So I. M. directs the building of the pyramid to begin
before the excavations beneath are finished.
Almost like building the roof of a house first.

When the mayor visits, he says,

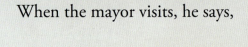

"Not bad."
The mayor's support softens the criticism.
Building eventually begins.

After a meeting with I. M., the mayor of Paris proposes setting up a full-size mock-up of the pyramid to help the public imagine what it could be. Over a few days, thousands view the model.

So, during difficult newspaper and TV interviews, he focuses his energy on the Confucian teachings his grandfather taught him.
  Never show anger.
  Express oneself calmly and clearly.
  Be patient.

I. M. knows that sometimes people don't like change.
However, he strongly believes that
"success is a collection of problems solved."
And his current problem to solve
is to gain the trust of the people of Paris.

And later, when his designs
of sleek, modern buildings
were viewed as too unusual,
he often faced criticism and doubts
until the structures were completed.

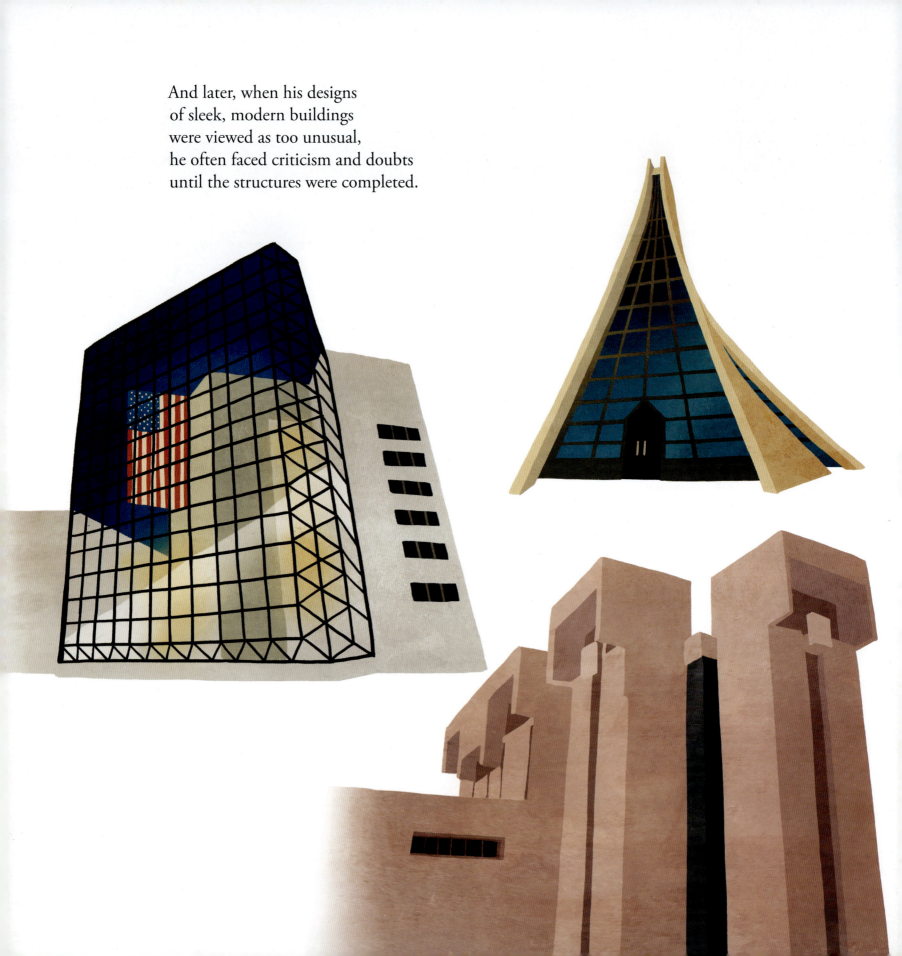

Refusing to back down, I. M. draws strength by recalling the many challenges he has overcome. When he first arrived in the US as a college student, he struggled with feeling like an outsider, sometimes facing discrimination for being Asian.

Ready to unveil his design,
I. M. believes the French public will love it.
He's wrong.
For months, the French call the pyramid names—

The ancient stone pyramids in Egypt were for the dead, built as tombs for mummies.
This modern glass pyramid in Paris will be for the living; a serene, sunlit space welcoming all visitors.

That's it!
I. M. sees a solution
rooted in the designs of gardens,
both French and Chinese.
The new entrance to the Louvre should be . . .

An enormous pyramid!
A pyramid of glass that will reflect
the glittering sun and the ever-changing Paris skies.
A glass pyramid that won't block views of the magnificent Louvre.
A pyramid that will seem to grow out of the courtyard.

Thinking of gardens, I. M. fondly recalls
his family's retreat in Suzhou, China,
where his ancestors lived for over six hundred years.
While his elders studied calligraphy and Chinese philosophy,
I. M. played hide-and-seek with his cousins
in the ancient Lion Grove Garden.
The children dashed by enormous rocks
shaped over years by streaming water
and then "planted" by esteemed rock gardeners.

Wanting to understand French designs, I. M. studies books about a famous garden at a French palace, Versailles, that features open space, light, water, and geometric shapes.

When I. M. works on creating a new design,
he thinks in Chinese, the language of his childhood.
When he creates possibilities in his mind,
his hands move in front of him
as if sketching in the air.
He sleeps badly and becomes irritable.
But he keeps trying.

He must think more, in deep silence.
The type of silence he experienced as a boy
when he traveled with his mother
to Buddhist retreats in the mountains of China.
The quiet was so complete,
I. M. was certain he could hear bamboo growing
in the nearby groves.

But what type of entry could it be?
Not a large structure that blocks the view
of the splendid walls of the Louvre.
Not a low tunnel opening that doesn't feel grand.
How can I. M. overcome this challenge?

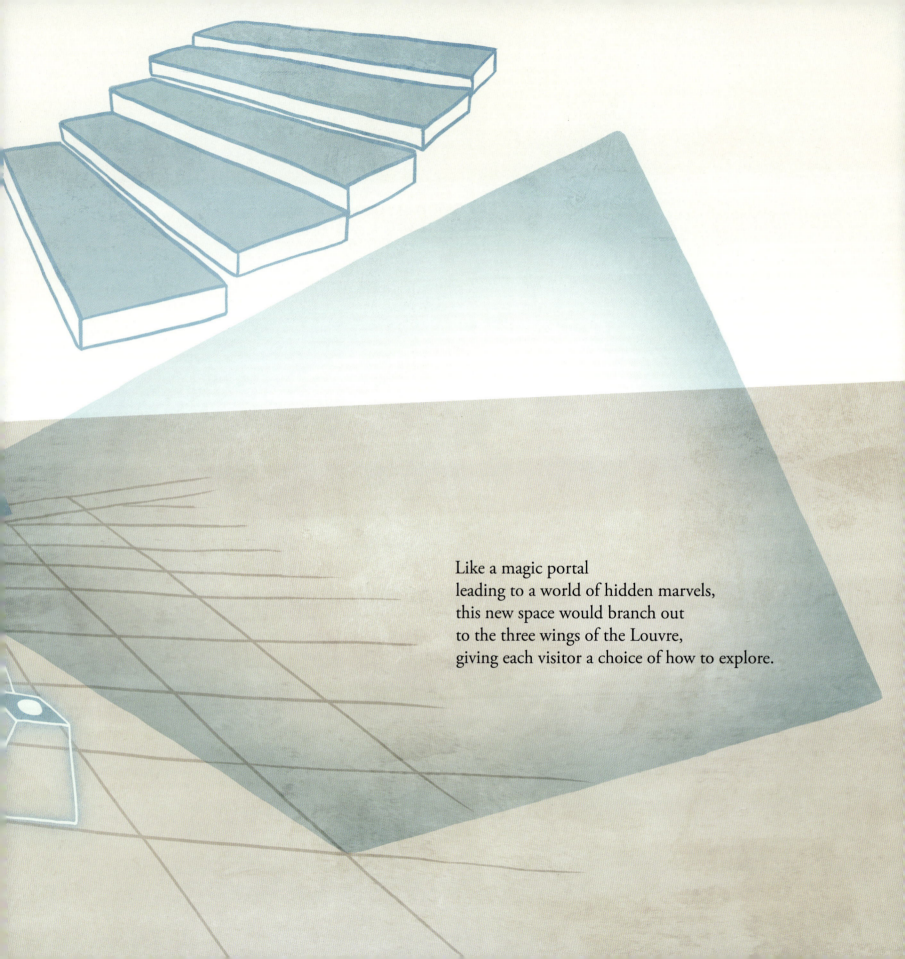

Like a magic portal
leading to a world of hidden marvels,
this new space would branch out
to the three wings of the Louvre,
giving each visitor a choice of how to explore.

What if the entrance to the Louvre
is no longer just a door on the building?
What if visitors could somehow enter the museum
from the large outside courtyard,
currently a dismal gravel parking lot?

Walking down lengthy hallways, he sees how visitors must undertake a tiresome trek from the entrance to reach the artworks.

And then I. M. has a seed of an idea!

I. M. investigates the galleries of the Louvre, admiring precious paintings and sculptures and relics from ancient times.

The French president chose I. M. Pei,
knowing he would not only respect
the history of the Louvre
but also create a modern space
that welcomes everyone.
Just as he had done with his addition
to the historic National Gallery of Art
in Washington, DC.

Now, as a museum, the Louvre,
gorgeous on the outside,
has problems inside.
Visitors struggle to find the entrance
and their way around the galleries.
Public space is sparse.
And no rooms to store or restore art pieces.

During the past eight hundred years, the Louvre has been a fortress, military barracks, a prison, and a palace for many kings— all before becoming a museum.

I. M. travels from his New York City office to soak up the beauty and culture of France. He studies the Louvre for weeks.

The French take great pride in the Louvre.
And they won't like an outsider
touching their national treasure.
I. M. worries that if word gets out
that he, a foreigner, is working on a plan
to change the beloved Louvre,
the project will be blocked.
So he tells no one.

IEOH MING ("I. M.") PEI

is on a secret mission.
He is a well-known architect,
a designer of important buildings.
And now the president of France
has offered I. M. the opportunity of a lifetime—
to redesign the famous Louvre,
the largest museum in the world
and home to the *Mona Lisa*.

THE GLASS PYRAMID

A Story of the Louvre Museum and Architect I. M. Pei

JEANNE WALKER HARVEY

ILLUSTRATED BY KHOA LE

Atheneum Books for Young Readers
NEW YORK LONDON TORONTO SYDNEY NEW DELHI

To Ron, mon amour
—J. W. H.

To Auntie Mai, thank you for my
first unforgettable trip to
the Louvre and Paris, a long time ago
—K. L.

ATHENEUM BOOKS FOR YOUNG READERS • An imprint of Simon & Schuster Children's Publishing Division • 1230 Avenue of the Americas, New York, New York 10020 • Text © 2025 by Jeanne Walker Harvey • Illustration © 2025 by Khoa Le • Photographs on p. 38: left: © Bernard Bisson; right: Photographs in the Carol M. Highsmith Archive, Library of Congress, Prints and Photographs Division • All rights reserved, including the right of reproduction in whole or in part in any form. • ATHENEUM BOOKS FOR YOUNG READERS is a registered trademark of Simon & Schuster, LLC. • Atheneum logo is a trademark of Simon & Schuster, LLC. • For information about special discounts for bulk purchases, please contact Simon & Schuster Special Sales at 1-866-506-1949 or business@simonandschuster.com. • The Simon & Schuster Speakers Bureau can bring authors to your live event. For more information or to book an event, contact the Simon & Schuster Speakers Bureau at 1-866-248-3049 or visit our website at www.simonspeakers.com. • The text for this book was set in Adobe Garamond. • The illustrations for this book were rendered digitally. • Manufactured in China • 0125 SCP • First Edition • 10 9 8 7 6 5 4 3 2 1 • Library of Congress Cataloging-in-Publication Data • Names: Harvey, Jeanne Walker, author. | Le, Khoa, 1982- illustrator. • Title: The glass pyramid : a story of the Louvre Museum and architect I. M. Pei / Jeanne Walker Harvey ; illustrated by Khoa Le. • Description: First edition. | New York : Atheneum Books for Young Readers, 2025. | Audience: Ages 4 to 8. | Summary: Despite discrimination and other challenges, architect I. M. Pei works on a secret mission to redesign the Louvre Museum and transform it into a welcoming place. • Identifiers: LCCN 2024005426 | ISBN 9781665953337 (hardcover) | ISBN 9781665953344 (ebook) • Subjects: LCSH: Pei, I. M., 1917-2019—Juvenile literature. | Musée du Louvre—Juvenile literature. | CYAC: Pei, I. M., 1917-2019—Fiction. | Louvre (Museum)—Fiction. | Chinese Americans—Fiction. | Architecture—Fiction. | Art museums—Fiction. | LCGFT: Picture books. • Classification: LCC PZ7.H26756 Gl 2025 | DDC [E]—dc23 • LC record available at https://lccn.loc.gov/2024005426

THE GLASS PYRAMID

What began as I. M.'s secret Louvre project
blossomed into a cherished symbol of France.
In the splendid garden of Paris,
Ieoh Ming Pei patiently planted
and then grew
a glorious glass pyramid.

WHAT DOES AN ARCHITECT DO?

An architect is a person who designs buildings and prepares plans to give to a builder. They make drawings with pens, pencils, and computers. Sometimes they make scaled-down models to show what the building will look like when it is done. Architects decide the size, shape, and materials of a building. They not only need to be good at math and drawing, but they also need imagination, creativity, and an understanding of what will make a building appealing and functional for the people who will be using it.

BRIEF BIOGRAPHY OF I. M. PEI

Ieoh Ming (I. M.) Pei was born in Guangzhou, China, in 1917. At the age of seventeen, he came to the United States to study architecture at MIT and Harvard University. He became a US citizen in 1954 and did not return to China until the mid-1970s, when he was commissioned to design a hotel in Beijing. Known for clean, modernist lines in his designs, he was famous for numerous large-scale architectural and planning projects in the US and throughout the world, including the modernization of the Louvre in Paris and the design of the East Building of the National Gallery in Washington, DC.

He received numerous honors and awards, including the Presidential Medal of Freedom, the Pritzker Architecture Prize, and the National Medal of Arts from the National Endowment for the Arts. In 2017, the American Institute of Architects bestowed the Twenty-five Year Award to I. M. Pei's renovation of the Louvre. The prize is given annually to a building that "has stood the test of time for twenty-five to thirty-five years and continues to set standards of excellence for its architectural design and significance." The Louvre Pyramid was inaugurated in 1989. I. M. Pei died in New York City in May 2019 at the age of 102.

LOUVRE PYRAMID
PARIS, FRANCE

NATIONAL GALLERY OF ART'S EAST BUILDING
WASHINGTON, DC

STEM CONNECTIONS: SOLVING CONSTRUCTION PROBLEMS

The square base of the glass Louvre Pyramid has sides measuring about 112 feet each. The height of the pyramid is 71 feet from the tip down to the center of the base. The pyramid has 673 glass panes—603 diamond shapes and 70 triangle shapes. I. M. Pei and his team needed to tackle numerous problems and difficulties in the construction of the Louvre Pyramid. Here's how they addressed some of the challenges.

CREATING THE GLASS

I. M. Pei wanted the glass to be very clear so that the views of the Louvre building would not be altered. A historic French glass company researched and developed a way to manufacture a special glass without iron impurities, such as iron oxides, which give glass a green tint.

CONNECTING THE GLASS PANES

The I. M. Pei team constructed a complicated metal structure of steel (weighing over 209,000 pounds) with an aluminum frame (weighing over 231,000 pounds). The challenge was connecting the glass panes to the sturdy metal skeleton. An unlikely source was used to design the cable system—a small rigging company in Massachusetts that worked on yachts for the America's Cup sailing competition.

The glass panels and the metal framework are connected by 2,150 stainless steel nodes. The overall system makes the entire structure both sturdy and flexible, and able to handle forces such as wind and temperature variations.

CLEANING THE GLASS PYRAMID

Cleaning the windows of tall buildings is difficult enough, but regular methods like scaffolding could not be used for the 71-foot-high structure of the Louvre Pyramid. So instead, after the pyramid was completed, mountaineers were hired to scale the slopes and clean the glass. Eventually, a small "breadbox–sized" robot was invented in 2002 to clean the pyramid. Maneuvered by remote control, the robot is secured to the glass via suction cups and has a squeegee and rotating brushes. However, some tasks are impossible to automate. Ropers are still used to repair the joints.

SELECTED SOURCES

Bezombes, Dominique. *The Grand Louvre: History of a Project*. Translated by Catherine Bergeron. Paris: Le Moniteur and Établissement Public du Grand Louvre, 1994.

Cannell, Michael. *I. M. Pei: Mandarin of Modernism*. New York: Clarkson Potter, 1995.

d'Archimbaud, Nicholas. *Louvre: Portrait of a Museum*. New York: Stewart, Tabori & Chang, 1998.

Jodidio, Philip. *I. M. Pei: La Pyramide du Louvre/The Louvre Pyramid*. Munich: Prestel, 2009.

Reid, Aileen. *I. M. Pei*. Albany: Knickerbocker, 1995.

Rubalcaba, Jill. *I. M. Pei: Architect of Time, Place, and Purpose*. New York: Marshall Cavendish, 2011

von Boehm, Gero. *Conversations with I. M. Pei: Light is the Key*. Munich: Prestel, 1999.

Wiseman, Carter. *I. M. Pei: A Profile in American Architecture*. New York: Abrams,1990.

ONLINE VIDEOS/INTERVIEWS

"*60 Minutes* Interview of I. M. Pei" (1987). Interviewed by Diane Sawyer during the construction stage of the Louvre Pyramid, and he also discussed other works. https://www.youtube.com/watch?v=y6DIeXWzSPw.

"Designing the Louvre Pyramid"—MIT Technology Day (1994). Interview of I. M. Pei with transcript. https://infinite.mit.edu/video/i-m-pei-designing-louvre-pyramid"-mit-technology-day-641994.

First person singular: I. M. Pei (2011). PBS documentary. https://www.youtube.com/watch?v=AxEIkWu03S8